T0365344

Farewell

AuthorHouse™ UK
1663 Liberty Drive
Bloomington, IN 47403 USA
www.authorhouse.co.uk
Phone: 0800.197.4150

Published by AuthorHouse   01/30/2019

ISBN: 978-1-5462-9809-0 (sc)
ISBN: 978-1-5462-9808-3 (e)

Library of Congress Control Number: 2018913272

Print information available on the last page.

authorHOUSE®

I dedicate this book to the memory
of my husband William Farwell
and to our children,
Claire, Bryony and Matthew.

The Contents

An Early Memory

Wartime, in the blackout
A crowded smoky train,
Laden with soldiers and civilians
Going to Liverpool.

There was an old woman sat
Disapprovingly opposite us
In the dark, dingy carriage.

My Father gave my young brother
Sips of his beer.
She sniffed, then scolded him roundly-
My Father laughed,

My Mother did not, neither did I-
No one offered a sip!.
The journey was endlessly wearisome to a child.

Night Comfort

My dolls and I lay at night
Together, in the great bed.
I lovingly placed them, newly dressed,
Six or eight, in order of size, laid on their backs.
I slept in the middle,
Safely-

When I had climbed into the bed, sliding carefully into the small cool place
There was just room.
The dolls smiled brightly up at the ceiling.
I had to stay quite still, or, I was poked by hard porcelain hands,
Hard round baby faces, with bright blue eyes, hard round bodies, short fat legs
I was squashed by them and could only be, on my back.

In the morning, I would wake, pull the ugly, black curtains
That kept out the morning sunshine.
I would leave my babies
Until the next night.

Where they would be quietly waiting, to be dressed
Smoothed and tucked into place once more
To dream-
Safely, thro' the night.

Square white room

Square, white painted room.
Nudes and still lifes – on the walls.
Silence, people are concentrating.
Hear brain ticking. Feel brain working
Slowly, slowly.

Door closing, someone enters, talking –
Silence again –
Pencils scratching the paper,
Paper rustles ---
Hear someone breathing,
Feel my hear thumping

So, am still alive,
Just.
Silence complete
Pictures on the wall
Still life and nudes,
In a square white room

The Conker Season

There was a season for each game.
One day, my brothers would wake up, go to school,
And come home with satchels and pockets stuffed with conkers.

So beautiful, laid on the kitchen table, smelling of autumn;
Dark mahogany polished to perfection by elfin creatures.
We looked at them with love and handled them with care.
My brothers examined each nut carefully, looking for the prize.
This year it would be found.

The chosen ones, would be dried slowly min front of the fire
Then a skewer was pushed through the nut
String was knotted, threaded, and they were ready.
My brother knew, if it was the right day and
They were carefully carried to school in satchels heavy with books,
The Champions were held at play time,
Discussions, on the walk home.

Sometimes, they were winners – this was really exciting,
Sometimes they lost – this was not talked about.
"Next Year", they sighed! The game was over
Winners and losers, the conker season was over
Winners and losers, the conker season was over
And the next game would be winter.

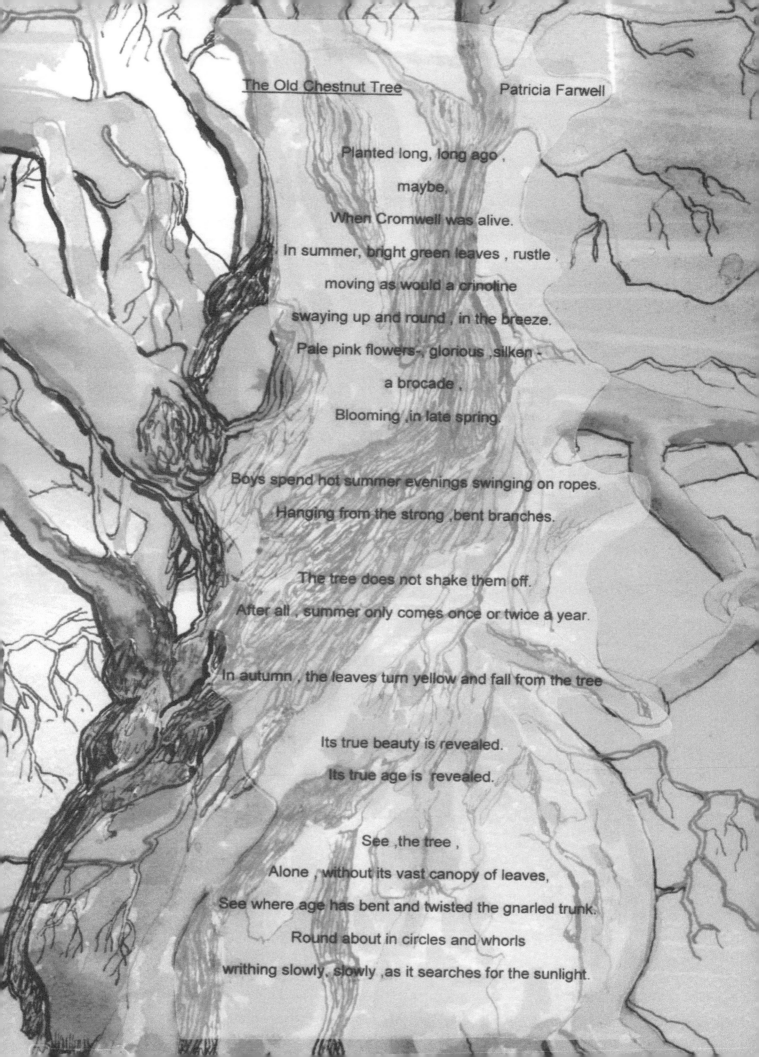

The Old Chestnut Tree   Patricia Farwell

Planted long, long ago ,

maybe,

When Cromwell was alive.

In summer, bright green leaves , rustle ,

moving as would a crinoline

swaying up and round , in the breeze.

Pale pink flowers-, glorious ,silken -

a brocade ,

Blooming ,in late spring.

Boys spend hot summer evenings swinging on ropes.

Hanging from the strong ,bent branches.

The tree does not shake them off.

After all , summer only comes once or twice a year.

In autumn , the leaves turn yellow and fall from the tree

Its true beauty is revealed.

Its true age is revealed.

See ,the tree ,

Alone , without its vast canopy of leaves,

See where age has bent and twisted the gnarled trunk.

Round about in circles and whorls

writhing slowly, slowly ,as it searches for the sunlight.

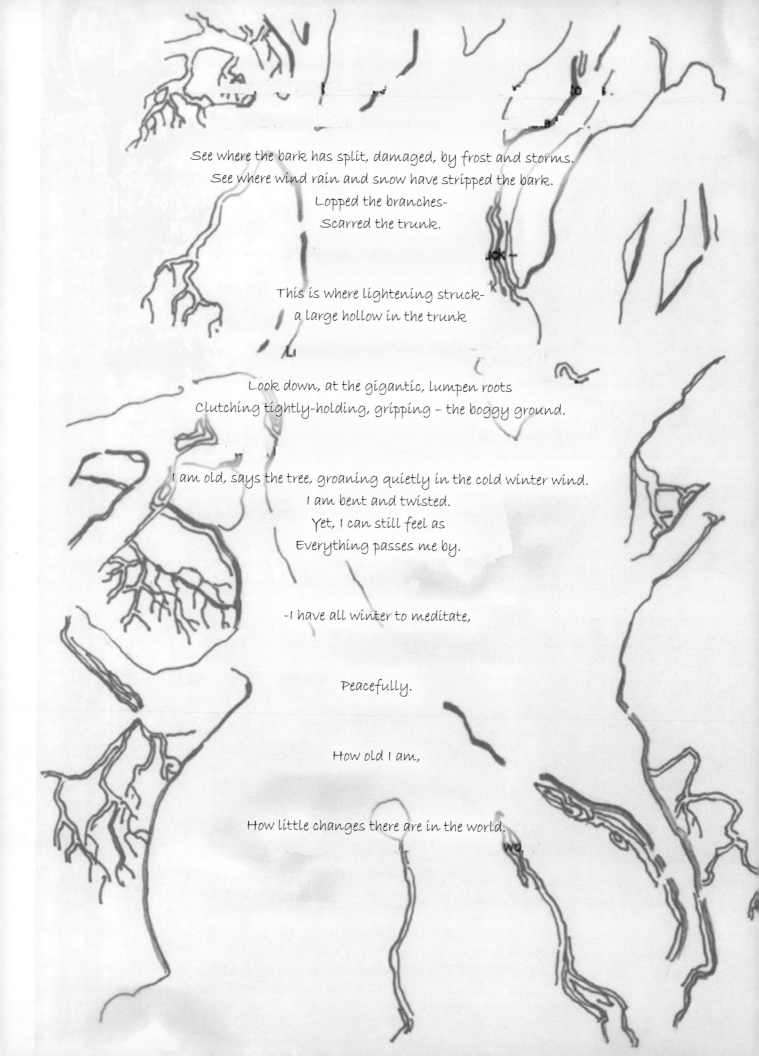

See where the bark has split, damaged, by frost and storms.
See where wind rain and snow have stripped the bark.
Lopped the branches-
Scarred the trunk.

This is where lightening struck-
a large hollow in the trunk

Look down, at the gigantic, lumpen roots
Clutching tightly-holding, gripping – the boggy ground.

I am old, says the tree, groaning quietly in the cold winter wind.
I am bent and twisted.
Yet, I can still feel as
Everything passes me by.

-I have all winter to meditate,

Peacefully.

How old I am,

How little changes there are in the world.

The Beech Wood

The vast silvery trunks of the beech trees
Stand silently in the soft leafy ground.
That rustles as you walk along.
I watch, as the leaves fall silently down
Drifting in the autumnal breeze.
Tyr to catch one as it falls. For every leaf you catch –
Next year – if you jeep it carefully,
You will have a lucky day.

Waiting at the school gate you made a vow that you would be really nice to the children today

Waiting at the Gate

Out they come, last as usual.
'Have you had lovely day?'
'Say hello to baby no baby you can't walk today-we're in a hurry!'
'Oh my goodness! – children, blow you noses'
Properly, properly, like this
Don't sniff, blow-
    That's better-
    Now you can breathe.

STOP, wait at the kerb-
WAIT, don't forget to look
Oh the car's stopping, it's missed.
You didn't look,
No, you didn't.
NOW, hold onto the pram and walk properly.
    Stop pulling down.

Did you have a nice day?
What did you have for your dinner?
WHO – ate your dinner?
The boy next to you!
    I KNOW-, You were pushing the food round the plate again
    You were playing with your food.

Well, tomorrow you had better eat faster.
Yes, he was a greedy boy
But if you had eaten the food he couldn't have had yours
It would have been in your stomach.
Remember that!

Now do blow your nose again.
We are crossing the road,
Hold onto the pram, cars are coming – don't run – walk.
Right, NOW you can run
Fast as you can
All of you,
Hurry, we've got a lot to do.

Try to walk properly,
Not with you head screwed round,
LOOK WHERE YOU'RE GOING!!!
Now you've tripped, never mind,
We'll put a plaster on when we get home,
it's not bleeding much.
Wipe the dog muck from your boots –
On the grass,
Over there – that's right. Stop pushing your sister,
Go round her – not over.

We're nearly home

Five Norman Churches

Visiting my brother in Gloucestershire, we discovered,

Five, utterly charming, 'Norman Churches, so small, that no more than maybe,

20 souls could worship there, at any one time.

Painted on the whitewashed walls, were the original, medieval murals;

Telling of the life of Jesus, His crucifixion and how He rose from the dead.

And through His sacrifice, after death, we may live forever in the Kingdom of God.

Left for a thousand years and by a miracle overlooked,

When Cromwell and his men, during the Civil War.

Rampaged, throughout the countryside, to destroy all traces of Catholicism.

These tiny churches have some pews for people and an Altar at the Eastern end, Still used for services.

Later, at home, we wrote to the Vicar in charge of these parishes.

He sent a map, drawn by himself, showing how the churches were placed in relationship to each and

the landscape and the pathways that joined the buildings.

There was the Devil chasing an Angel along the paths, shouting,

'May the Devil take the hindmost'-but,

The Devil never quite caught the angel-----yet!

Memories of the generations of people worshipping here, were almost visible

One felt, surrounded, protected by the love and simple faith so alive in this place.

No carved tombs, ceilings, walls, choir stalls, Silver and Gold, treasures, riches

Worth a fortune in this temporal world, But an air of quiet contemplation.

The murals telling the old, old stories painted by devoted, unknown, keepers of the faith.

When we returned to the house of my brother

We excitedly told his family what we had witnessed

They had not heard of these churches.

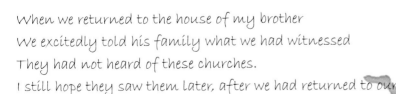

I still hope they saw them later, after we had returned to our home.

Autumn Walk in the Woods

The wood is golden, I walk
Watching the leaves fall from the trees.
Twirling, fluttering, down they come.
I try to catch them – missing –
They gently touch the ground
To join the thousand million leaves already fallen
Over the centuries.

I tell the children, 'hurry, catch a leaf for luck.'
'That's easy', they shout-
And start running
To catch them
Floating down, in the light breeze.

'It's not easy', they cry – darting
After the fickle yellow and orange leaves.

'Try again and again',
'You will catch one, or maybe two,'
'You will have a lucky day next year.'
You can't have too many,

'Keep them carefully.'
'For when they may be needed.'

The Abandoned Cottage

I have no home now.
I walk on lonely roads in the country side, where
The scenery is wonderful, mountains, trees, water, grass.
The Weather changes,
Dry, wet, cold, hot, sunshine, rain, mist, fog, snow, hail,
Ceaselessly different.

I pass the cottage.
Perhaps I can stay here for a while-
Light a fire, warm myself, cool a simple meal.
I will trap a rabbit, stew in my pot, with the wild herbs and cabbage
I found growing by the broken door.
I wrap myself in my worn blanket,
Skin the rabbit, on a stone slab
Then cook, slowly, - I am ready to eat my fill –

I am very content,
And drift away in sleepy happiness.

Suddenly –
I awaken; - all has been a dream
And I am cold, damp, frozen to the bone –
And sitting in one wet grass by the roadside
Looking at the cottage
In the distance.

I have no home.

The Curse Sorter

I am a curse sorter
I will tell you about them my dears.

I also deal in Oath, long repulsive and dangly ones
I will create one just for you.
For a special occasion, needing a particular oath-
Also, everyday curses
That everyone curses
That everyone uses –
"God in heaven, look down on me and curse the day that I was born!
"I'll go to the foot of our stairs,"
"Dang me! – strewth man! stone the crows!"
"May you rot in hell!' "Geeze"!!!!!
'Fire and brimstone!'
'Not worth a curse, worth nothing not worth a fig'

Hot flames lick the stones of the hearth –
I can smell the Vulcan fire embers, feel the heat thr' my thick, black, wool robe
I stir the words in a stew of wrath, the smoke burns my eyes,
The fires spit and rumble in the chimney-hissing, roaring squeling
Words pour in from everywhere.
Red, purple, passionate angers,
Rages that melt down into Hell
Unbearable is the room. –I am burning up.
I do like a ling drawn-black, black, spiraled oath at the end of a
Hard days work.

Then – I sleep well in my little white bed, after a good days cursing.

The Lesson

(The old Handbags)

I walked into the room one sunny afternoon,
The women were sitting in their wheelchairs waiting for me.
I was to be the treat that day;
They terrified me, old bodies, twisted by arthritis, strokes and old age
Like the gnarled trunks of trees.

'I can't spend a whole afternoon here!' panic was in my head.

They watched me, bright bird like eyes,
Clutching their battered handbags in their feeble, gnarled hands.
These they never let out of sight,
Until they were gently removed by the kinds hands of nurses, when they died.

Meanwhile, they weren't dead yet!
'What have you come for to show us?'
'What are we gangin 'tae dae?'

If they could see, their hands didn't work –
If their hands worked, their eyes had failed.
And all were slightly deaf.

I thought desperately—

I told them they could work in pairs, as a team
One could see, the other could paint.

They chatted brightly, constantly, they came alive to me.
I forgot their twisted bodies.
I could see their bright souls.
These women still had minds as sharp as razors
They watched me closely judged what I did and said what they thought.
'I used to be teacher', said one gently', you'll be good one day –
Given time!'
We had a nice sup of tea and a pause.
'She was a good teacher' said the others nodding, 'she taught oll our bairns to read.

'My baby is coming to visit today', said another,
'How old is your baby?' said I,
'Sixty next week'.

The baby walked in slowly, he was an old man.
She proudly introduced him to me, her baby, the youngest of eight.
I wondered how a baby could be so old.

Now I know.

First Love

We met
At my first dance
Where I was bored by a blind date
My Mother had arranged.
My Mother, asked Bill
To come and join us
As he was alone.

He was so beautiful,
I fell in love
Immediately.
And made big eyes
at him.

I was stunning in my new silk dress –
'Dance with me 'I murmured—
'Dance through life',
And the music played
Loudly and long
And we were moving
Alone in a crowd

Dancing through life.

Recipe for Life

Blend two people,
Marinate with life.
Fold in children,
Scatter them round
To mix with others.
Cool down with time.
Fold into earth.

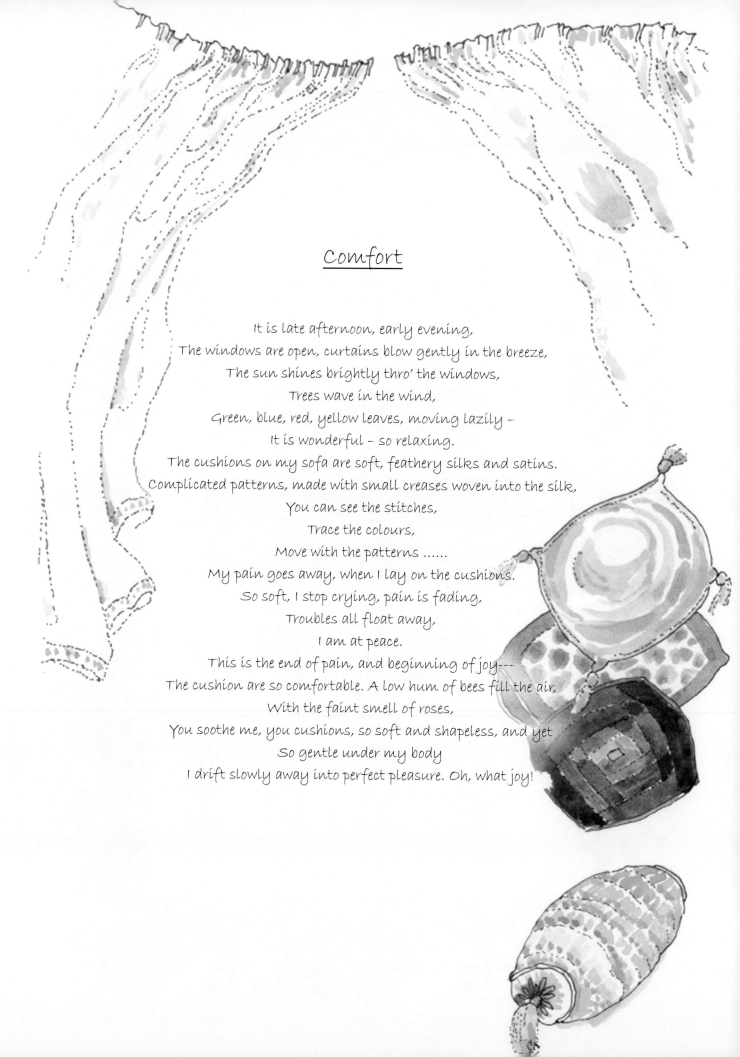

Comfort

It is late afternoon, early evening,
The windows are open, curtains blow gently in the breeze,
The sun shines brightly thro' the windows,
Trees wave in the wind,
Green, blue, red, yellow leaves, moving lazily –
It is wonderful – so relaxing.
The cushions on my sofa are soft, feathery silks and satins.
Complicated patterns, made with small creases woven into the silk,
You can see the stitches,
Trace the colours,
Move with the patterns ......
My pain goes away, when I lay on the cushions.
So soft, I stop crying, pain is fading,
Troubles all float away,
I am at peace.
This is the end of pain, and beginning of joy---
The cushion are so comfortable. A low hum of bees fill the air,
With the faint smell of roses,
You soothe me, you cushions, so soft and shapeless, and yet
So gentle under my body
I drift slowly away into perfect pleasure. Oh, what joy!

My Garden

My garden is beautiful.
My love is buried under the thorn tree
Which guards him through the years.
The honeysuckle grows through the hedge, ivy creeps along the ground
Covering the brown earth with a blanket of shiny new leaves.
The cherry tree, covered in red leaves.
Bullfinches eat the delicate white blossoms.
The Hawthorn, with pink flowers – hidden spikes scratch the unwary
Field Maple and the Acer, bright red leaves in Autumn. Rowan keep the witches away –
Mahonia has vicious viridian spikes.
There are the different hued Hollies
The Elderflowers growing in the Beech hedges – white frothy flowers and purple berries.
Spring flowers giving pleasure after the long, long hard winter.
Daffodils dance, crocus, hyacinths, primulas, cowslips, bluebells,
Give away to bleeding hearts, pansies, poppies, foxgloves, blowsy pink peonies,
Summer roses, scent the air.
Clematis, daisies, snapdragons,
Gorgeous curly ferns growing so fast-, so beautiful so delicate,
My love lies in the earth, near to me in my garden.
So near the flowers in summer – lying, dormant in the winter.
One day we will lie again, together again.

Frogs in Spring

The pond lay reflecting the cold spring sky.
Water moving, small ripples spread across the surface.
The water was heaving with frogs.
Faces smiling, the eyes bright with delight –
Frogs gathered in an intimate fashion, grouping in threes and twos.
They leapt up and down with excitement in the clear brown water.
At the edge against the fresh green weeds
Lay heaps of spawn, silvery jelly protecting the eggs
Frogs were croaking, "come and join, come and join".
More frogs hurried to the pond,
Time seems so short
And the party lasts for weeks.

It is spring again, hope the weather is mild
The tadpoles hatch, head grow fast, legs and arms pop out
New babies jump with the joy of life.

The adults forget the frenzy; idly they swim in the water,
Waiting for the next spring.

My Spine

My spine is the old man of the sea
He clings to me; hurting, as he presses down on me.
My spine screams with a hurricane of pain –
My spine is a frosty morning. Icy cold.
My spine is a moaning, groan, carrying on – forever
Whining and grinding.
My spine is dreary grey – dull and dreak!
My spine is rocky, stiff and steep to climb
Handholds are hard to find – to grip.
My spine is a tortoise, slow to move, boney and old
My spine is a badly built 60's tower block. Run down and tatty,
Darkly dangerous full of unknown terrors,
Nasty things happen, around dark corners.
My spine is a wire coat hanger used to hang my bones, my shoulders and head
Bent, and brittle twisted with time and use.

<u>To reply to my letter of March 2011-03-29</u>

Dear Patricia,

I am your back and am replying to your last letter which was sent March 2011.

You are always sending me letters, asking me why I behave as I do.

I behave as I do because I have no choice.

Some of the trouble is not your fault. It is genetic, a weak spine. A great deal is your fault!

You didn't take as much care of your spine as a child, or as an adult, as you should have done.

You used it carelessly.

You lived.

Climbed trees, swung from ropes, stood on our head, turned cartwheels, rolled on the ground,

fought with your brothers, rode bikes and ponies, swam, fell off walls, trees, danced

You used your back, non-stop!

You didn't always take care to sit straight, walk tall. You slouched in chairs,

moved furniture, lifted things without bending your knees.

Very careless!

You got pregnant, had babies, cleaned, cooked, dusted, stood for hours,

lifted children, pushed prams, washed china, clothes, children.

I could go on Etc. Etc.

Your back started to ache, but you ignored the pain and carried on doing what

you had always done. The pain went away, came back, went away again.

The cycle had begun

On you went, being careful when it hurt – doing what you wanted when it stopped.

Now it hurts all the time and you write and ask me why.

Now I have told you what you knew all along

Yours sincerely

Your ever faithful Spine.

The Newborn Baby

Yet another generation –
So small, so beautiful.
Full of hope for the future.
Will she
Grow up as beautiful, as she looks now
Maybe – maybe not.

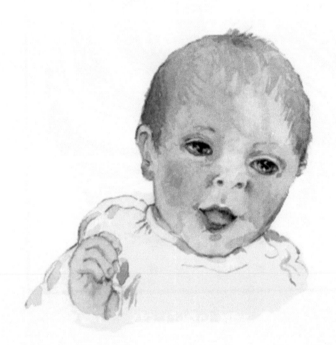

A little poem I wrote for Emily, on the occasion of her Christening, which I enclose, with love.
I am sending the Bible, which belonged to her Grandfather, William Talbot Lang Farwell.

Waves on The Beach

Standing alone on the beach, I can see the tide is coming in.
The waves mesmerize me, one after the other they pound the sand and shingle.
They crash, the wind howls in my ears, cold and bitter.
I am warm in my thick coat and boots.

I am losing awareness of everything but the sea coming closer yet closer
I cannot move

The waves are large dark, green, shiny with foam, dangerous –
The single gull whirls and screams as it passes – riding on the wind –
I can hear nothing but the sound of the water – the sound of
the wind – the scream of the gull high above
My brain is filled with noise. Everything else is wiped away
My head is clear,

There is a mist of water on my face and hair and I can taste the salt on my lips.
I feel nothing but the elements, pushing, pulling me into the water.
Come with me into the water, into the waves.
Let the wind blow on into the waves, wash away in the water
Let the wind blow me into the air and fly with the gull above the wet, watery, waves.

I slip in the water and all is silence. Peace.

A Creature in the Forest

The night was very cold. Freezing rain was falling.

The night was dark, black, black as coal. Black and wet. The kind of rain that penetrates to your very heart. To your very soul.

I am walking, and I am so tired. I have been walking for hours, my legs hurt, my whole body hurts. I know that I cannot go much further. I must find somewhere to take shelter, try to get warm. To wait for morning.

I must find shelter.

Where am I going?

I don't know where I am. In these woods I am lost. I am alone. I am haunted by the trees standing silently round me, tall, dark, and sinister. I feel they are expecting something to happen, but what? Are they watching, guarding their privacy, driving me out into the open countryside?

I must keep moving.

I think I am being followed, I feel that I am being watched, strange eyes are keeping their gaze on me. Dreadful things are about to happen, I am so scared, so frightened.

I must not panic, for then all will be lost. I must not panic. I must keep calm – I try to breathe deeply but it is difficult, as the cold is making me shiver and my terror is growing, growing by the minute. The rain is driving shards of ice into my veins.

My boots are cut to pieces, and blood is running out of my feet. The warm blood turns cold as it lays in my boots, between my toes, under my soles. My feet freeze as the blood lies in my socks.

My heart is beating loudly. I can hear nothing but the beating of my heart. I will never find my way …

Suddenly I hear a noise – Ah … is it my imagination? It must be my imagination --- I try to hold my breath, to hear better over the noise of my thundering heart.

Don't panic, no one knows that I am here. What shall I do? What is happening? Who is there?

There is another cracking sound, someone stepped on a twig. Nonsense, I tell myself sternly. There is no one. No one knows where I am –

I don't know where I am.

I must not panic I must not panic. I can now feel my breathing, so loud, in the cold air. I am sure that anyone could hear it, so loud does my breath come and go. My hear is banging like a drum ... Shh ... what is it?

I hear another crack, like a rifle shot, close behind.

Panic is rising. I start to run, but seem to move so very slowly. I must be careful not to trip on tree roots. The ground is soft and boggy. The ground is clutching at my ankles. Why are they coming, what do they want? I know well it is me they want.

I cannot escape.

Which direction to run in? I must go forward because I feel someone is there behind me, getting closer. I keep going forward, stumbling and sobbing. Trying to run faster and not succeeding.

There is another sound. This time though, I can barely hear it over the noise of my heart beating.

A sound like the big bass drum.

My heart feels it will burst out of my chest. Louder this time, Dum, dum, dum, goes my heart. The blood is roaring my ears, there is a heavy pain in my chest. I fall over a root that is sticking out of the ground.

I trip again.

This time, I cannot rise. I can only lay there hearing my heavy panting breath, gasping,

Panic envelopes me, I cannot rise.

Who is it? Who is there?

There is no answer in the dark.

Just silence in the woods.

A creature in the forest

Falling, sleety snow, so cold. Slipping into the dark forest
I stumble on the rough, leaf strewn ground. I am lost, alone.
Who is watching, dark and sinister.
Trees move, creaking, moaning in the wind.
Shivering, I move onwards.
The snow is diving icy shards into my veins
And blood runs from my damaged feet. They freeze and
My heart thunders. I hear nothing but my heart ...
I try to hold my breath,
Who, who is following behind?

Nobody knows I am here,
That I am lost – lost in these endless woods.

There is a sound – a crack - close behind – I try to run, but ...
I try to hold my breath,
Who, who is following behind?

Nobody knows I am here,
Then I am lost – lost in these endless woods.

There is a sound – a crack-close behind – I try to run, but,
The roots clutch at my ankles
I stumble --- there is,
A terrible scream, such a noise!
Blood is roaring in my ears, pounding,
A heavy pain, in my chest,
I trip, fall, cannot rise.
Who is it? What is there?
There is no answer.

Just silence in the woods.

Haiku

Bare branches – pale leaves
Darken in summer, turn red,
Fall. Trees bare and black.

Watery sunshine,
Bare, frost covered branches,
Glisten in the light.

Stark against the sky,
Frost covered branches
Glisten in the night.

Haiku

Yellow green daisies
Gently moving in the soft
Scented summer breeze.

Gold and silver fish
Under the water lilies
Slowly glide around.

Wind whistles over
The rippling water. Sunshine
Sparkles on the wave tips.

Gold and silver fish
Drift lazily thro' the weeds
Slipping lightly by.

A Poem for Old Age

He stood in the doorway,

Looked mournfully at his wife,

"Come for a walk," he murmured.

She rose, and hand in hand, they strode towards the setting sun.

Now, in the autumn of their lives,

On a weekly trip to the Chemist.

Where they collected the carrier bags,

Containing the drugs, given to keep them alive.

Pills to help you rise,

To make you sleep,

To help you walk,

To get you going,

To stop you going,

To aid your thinking,

To make you care.

So you no longer care!

Later on, in the evening, they opened all the boxes,

And on the big table, by the window.

Arranged, two lines of seven pills

One line for each. Seven times a day, they stood.

Side by side, each with a pill to take-in water-

Green pills_purple pain pills,

Yellow pills-orange head pills,

Long white pills that might!

Small round red pills for the night!

Even blue and orange pills, to make one glad, not sad,

So, a week passed

Then, one afternoon

He stood in the doorway again,

And, looking mournfully at his wife and said_

"Do you fancy a walk to the Chemist?"

And, hand in hand, they strolled in the sunset,

Into the autumn of their lives.

Spring was gone, summer too_

Winter snarled in the distance.

But, now, in the Autumn of their lives,

A beautiful red and gold sunset.

In the autumn of their lives.

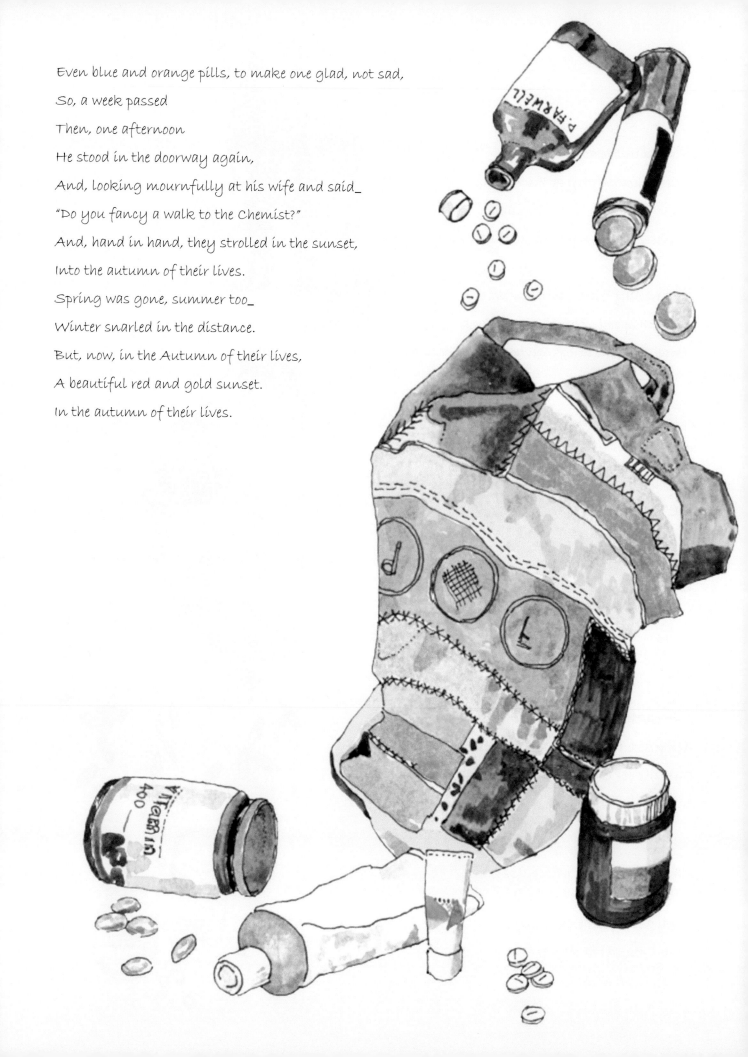

Printed in the United States
By Bookmasters